Terrible Terrain

Terrible Terrain

Jean LeBlanc

poems inspired by the life of lavinia dickinson

SHANTI ARTS PUBLISHING
BRUNSWICK, MAINE

Terrible Terrain Flowers

Copyright © 2023 Jean LeBlanc

All Rights Reserved
No part of this document may be reproduced or transmitted in any form or by any means without prior written permission of the publisher, except in the case of brief quotations embodied in critical reviews.

Published by Shanti Arts Publishing

Designed by Shanti Arts Designs

Cover and interior images are the work of the author and are used with her permission.

Shanti Arts LLC
193 Hillside Road
Brunswick, Maine 04011
shantiarts.com

Printed in the United States of America

ISBN: 978-1-956056-75-4 (softcover)

Library of Congress Control Number: 2023931361

In memory of Rita T. Mallahy,
teacher, friend,
and lover of all things Dickinson

Contents

First Riddle • 15
They Tell Me I Was a Problem Child • 16
Millrace • 17
Sitting for Our Portrait by Mr. O. A. Bullard, Itinerant Painter • 18
When I Die • 20
The Cemetery from My Bedroom Window • 21
A Man O' War in Full Sail • 22
Playing Jane Eyre • 24
An Amherst Rain • 25
Lines Inscribed on a Page in an Ecclesiastical History Text • 26
Sleepwalker • 27
Astronomy Notes • 28

Herbarium • 29
School Outing with Watercolors • 30
The Limits of Mother's Patience • 32
It Is Easy to Make Mother Leave the Room • 33
In Cambridge with Cousins Fanny and Lou • 34
Pioneer Valley • 35
Letter to Monsieur Daguerre • 36
You realize you have taken one step too many • 37
The Monson Ladies' Prayer Circle • 39
Emily Writes from School • 40
Knowing Emily • 41
The Binding is Spoiled by Placing the Open Book Pages-Down • 42

A Certain Kiss • 43

Sometimes She Goes Too Far • 44

First Loss • 45

Election • 46

Poor Maggie Tulliver • 47

When You Are Broken at Last • 48

Distance. Ways to Make It: • 49

This Morning Belongs • 50

Seek-no-furthers • 51

The Journey to Washington, D. C. • 52

Blasphemy • 53

Please, Visitor, Do Not Tell • 54

Fossils • 56

Embroidered Tapestry • 57

Imagining Emily • 58

Riddles • 59

Hard Freeze • 60

Variations • 62

Talking to Myself • 63

A Riddle for Sue • 64

Everything in Those Days Meant to Bind • 65

Ssshhh . . . merely whisper this: hankering, gross, mystical, nude • 66

"Emily, what does it mean?" • 68

Gaze for Which I Ceased to Live • 70

Gettysburg • 71

Alternate Words: Leaving/Staying • 72

Sense • 73

Samuel • 74

Abiah, with Dandelions in Her Hair • 76

Anachronism: What Was Wrong with Her? • 77

Riddles for Ned • 78

Fire in the Heart of Town • 80

Conversation with the Butcher • 81

Emily Bakes Gingerbread for Cousin Zebina, Which I Take to Him While Emily Sits with Mother • 82

Cousin Zebina's Paralysis • 83

What Can Be Found • 84

Prone to Outbursts • 85

The Yellow Day • 86

The Mushroom Girl • 87

Judge Otis Phillips Lord (1812–1884) • 88

After Burning All Her Letters • 89

April, 1886 • 90

Judgment Day • 92

When I Bathed Them • 93

Parts of Us • 94

Ordinary Deaths in an Ordinary Family • 95

In a Few Years, It Will Be the Twentieth Century • 96

And So It Is • 98

Summer, 1899 • 99

Acknowledgments

"Sleepwalker" and, in another form, "The Yellow Day" first appeared in *Where We Go: haiku and tanka sequences and other concise imaginings* (Modern English Tanka Press, 2010).

"Riddles" and "Conversation with the Butcher" appeared in *Community College Moment*, volume 17 (Lane Community College, 2017).

"In a Few Years, It Will Be the Twentieth Century," "Anachronism: What Was Wrong with Her," and "Gettysburg" appeared in *Community College Moment*, volume 18 (Lane Community College, 2018).

"Millrace" was made into a short film by animator Gal Cohen, part of the 2020 Moving Words project sponsored by ARTS by the People, Morristown, New Jersey.

"Letter to Monsieur Daguerre" and "Astronomy Notes" appeared in *Platform Review*, Autumn, 2021.

First Riddle

I am not the one. I am sister to the one.
Slightly off from what you were expecting.

I am not of this time. Neither are you,
really, or why would you be reading this?

I spend this life trying not to think too much
of the next. There is more than one next.

We all three started early, my two siblings and I.
I lasted the longest. I, who did so little of note,

destroyed too much. But what remains
remains because of me.

Do all somebodies worry about being nobody?
The answer to this riddle is a riddle.

They Tell Me I Was a Problem Child

For three months, four, six (the stories vary)
after my birth, mother could not bear to be
in the same room with me, could nearly
not bear to be in the same house. Babies
do not understand the sin of tears.
After six months, however, I was reformed
enough to be taken to church and baptized
for good measure, a little extra water
upon my face, a new beginning.

At this same time, my sister
was baptized by fire, during a lightning storm
while riding in a carriage with our aunt.
Neither the carriage nor its cargo was struck,
but when the very air is on fire
and one is in the open air, well.
It is a little something more than holy water
sprinkled on one's brow.

We have been water and fire ever since,
elemental siblings who mutually soothe
and spark, each a life force,
one without the other a certain catastrophe.

Millrace

On summer days the millrace fills with sky,
with whitest clouds against the bluest blue,
and up and down its length go dragonflies,

and all along its edge the catbirds cry,
and little ferns between the stones take root.
And though it isn't deep, this ribbon sky,

we have been told a thousand times to try
to stay back from its slippery sides, or rue
the day we'll fall. We're told so many lies,

you'd think the world is just a place to die.
It's hard and sharp and steep and slick and toothed,
but how could one fall downward into sky?

Another summer day, another try
at making time stand still, at naming blue,
at finding answers to our childish why—

And overhead the clouds go racing by,
and on the hottest days the stones are cool,
and up and down the millrace, dragonflies,
and reaching down into the water, sky.

Sitting for Our Portrait
by Mr. O. A. Bullard, Itinerant Painter

He means to help us keep still by talking,
but when he says things such as, "I paint
every face as if it were the first face
I've ever seen," Emily turns her head
toward the window and he must stop
and position us again just so.

Please do not paint my jacket too tight,
Austin says. We all three have a fear
of tight clothing.

One may grow to hate roses if one
is forced to hold them too long.

The sad hours, ignoring what falls from the sky.

At least we didn't have to hold the book of psalms.

Will our ears peek out of the gloom?

He tells us, "I will paint a subtle but fantastical background, one that hints at an ancient land where children are revered—"

"Where is that land?" the red-haired one inquires—

And then he forgets and says again, "I paint every face as if it were the last face I'll see."

Emily drops the book, drops the rose.

When I Die

Always a fly or two buzzing
in this house. Emily and I joke
that it is the same fly, summer
after summer, immortal.

Big bluebottle, resident of
the warm corner of the kitchen,
though sometimes seen strolling along
the bright glass of the conservatory.

Watcher at every deathbed,
guest at every wake, always
eyeing the refreshments.
The last sound we'll hear.

The Cemetery from My Bedroom Window

The world is all corners.
A temple for each heart.

A star fort from whose walls
the soldiers can fire upon those

who would attempt a breach.
Infrequent attempts at break-in here.

Once a week or so, someone new
takes the winding route through stone.

On the edge, the ones in black.
Mourners, I am told.

Gravel to grave they walk.
Gravel to grave and back.

I watch and wait. That, I remind myself,
is miracle enough.

A Man O' War in Full Sail

Then two, then a third—
three aunts descend
from the carriage

A pall settles over town
the parlor fills with skirts
the rustle and ruffle of it all

Emily's face like a bubble
about to burst

appalling how her spine curves forward

appalling her bitten nails

and then I cannot see to see
and then I am on my bed

bubble faces looking down at me

You fainted from the heat
Emily whispers in my ear
Was it quite thrilling, Dear, to die?

Playing Jane Eyre

Helen is kept home; her mother is dying, may die at any moment. Is dying and may die, both at once. Helen's younger sister Anne comes to play with us; it is Anne's birthday. With our dolls we re-enact Jane Eyre setting off on her own after Rochester's betrayal. Emily describes the loneliness of the moors, dragging her doll across interminable lengths of floorboard. Anne begins to cry. Jane will make it, she'll be all right, I tell her. But my mother will not, Anne replies. Even the doll stops at the thought, slumps over at the weight of it.

But no, that cannot be how it happened. Mrs. Fiske died in 1843. Jane Eyre did not come into our lives for several years after that. But I remember Anne, the doll, Emily saying something about the moors at night. What is it that fabricates memory so—"fabricates," another excellent word, I will not use it around Emily or she will steal it and insist it is hers. But memory, it might as well be imagination, for all its distinctions apart from fact. Perhaps it is easier to recover from loss, if one reminds oneself it is not memory, but imagination, that created that now-lost world.

An Amherst Rain

Thrilling to see the world
washed clean,

especially when one can watch
cleanliness transpire,

no need for one to do
the scrubbing oneself.

The rain knows best,
every intimate corner

of cobble and curb.
Only in the garden,

the next day, do I find
where the ground is still dry.

The way of mulch
is not the way of stone.

Lines Inscribed on a Page in an Ecclesiastical History Text

The children weep.
The sinners reap.
The lovers leap.
The elders sleep.
The angels keep.

Sleepwalker

All Amherst knows him. Even the horses
snort a low greeting from their stalls. Sometimes
he seems to have a little task in mind. Leave

a watering can full, and your roses will be tended
before dawn. Leave the broom by the back door,
your porch will be swept. If you thank him later,

he will shrug, not knowing what you mean.
Some mornings, we find him curled at the foot
of an elm. One of us carries him home, to bed.

Astronomy Notes

Our text begins with Adam,
amazed at the setting sun.

We learn the rules that bind
the planets to their planes,
and how, despite attractions,
order is maintained.

All the great names are here:
Copernicus, Galileo, Kepler,
Newton. My head aches
with law after law, the men
who make them.

Oh that there was such a thing
as retrograde.

We do not occupy the center—
Hipparchus taught us that.
What we call "irregularities"
are just our deficient points of view.

Observatories cannot disperse the clouds.

Herbarium

The page with the pink lady's-slipper orchid

That day in the late Spring woods

The dry and stony woods—well-drained as botanists say—
there they were, all these little ladies

who are quite common but seem so rare
—an orchid, after all, an orchid wild in New England—

Spring wears her slippers into summer

She is so good at the pressing, my sister
teasing the flower to flatten just so

half-humming
half coaxing as she works

I flatter it flat
she once said

Lives carefully pressed
arranged

fastened to a page
preserved forever

Evidence of what once was alive

School Outing with Watercolors

Mt. Holyoke, Sugar Loaf,
somewhere between the two
a little painted village
looks the same as it did
fifty, sixty years ago

depicted on our bright leaves:
the wind calm, the riverbend
never dammed with ice,
a hillside on fire
but only with setting sun,

just enough drama
to transport us to the realm
of romance, not to
the tragedy beyond.
One can see in these

amateur ambitions
such promise: we promise
that we'll all be home in time
without even missing
the blessing, the first course

we promise
nothing will change,
that jumble of gables
the one steeple
never felled by storm

and all storms pass, leaving behind
clouds of every conceivable color
and little daubs of paint
you can convince yourself
look like birds in flight.

The Limits of Mother's Patience

Grave and exotic—that is what Amherst is,
that is what this life is. Grave and exotic.

Mother says will I please stop using that word.
She means "grave," though "exotic" no doubt

displeases her as well. Her face goes all pinched
when I let it slip in the kitchen. I say,

"I must attend to the garden today, all those
spent roses crowding out the new buds,

how grave it all looks" and mother
leaves the room. Emily remains silent,
but she also remains by my side.

It Is Easy to Make Mother Leave the Room

Talk about the upcoming move. The work being done on the new house. The Homestead, new though not new (another riddle!), back in Father's charge, the Dickinson name cleared at last of the specter of bankruptcy. Bankruptcy! If I so much as whisper that word to Emily, Mother will fold the dish towel and abide in the kitchen no more.

But even without bankruptcy, discussion of the move makes mother go all formal, her posture indignant, braced against some invisible force. Perhaps from the cupola we can see all the way to Springfield, Emily says. From our rooms there shall be fields and hills. I know she is being brave; she dreads the move almost as much as Mother.

Could I possibly have heard one or the other of them say, "Moving is like a little death"?

Her mind leaves first, and soon her body follows.

In Cambridge with Cousins Fanny and Lou

I keep my letters sober, knowing that for her
this town was all needles, darkness,
poemless months, the smell of books,

the feel of them in her hand,
turning page after wordless page.
"She did that for hours," Lou says,

whispering at the memory. We compensate
with laughter, our commotion rising from
the cobbled streets, church bells humming

in sympathy. I write home: Mornings are gray
with mist. I do not say that when the sun
burns through, one can watch sailboats

own the river, one can smell the sea,
one can lift off and join the circling wheel
of gulls, up into the sea-bright sky,

drink in this light, feel it in one's
open mouth, taste it, fresh and
endless—but oh, no, dear sister,

you were right (I write), such shadows,
such dim corners, it would never do
to tarry here, to let one's eyes accustom.

Pioneer Valley

Adrift in the map, situated far
from any distinctive curve of coastline

farther still from
snowcapped range

yes we have our river
and our great broad valley

some wild wild hills
called "mountains" with a wink

(Just you try climbing one or two some morning,
says Miss Know-it-all of Holyoke Female Seminary)

I do not dispute these hills are too much
for the likes of me

but she has turned back to the window
compass and chart always ready to correct

as if she alone knows the straights and narrows
cartographer in petticoats

as if only she can see
the terrible terrain ahead

Letter to Monsieur Daguerre

Dear Sir—Do you have a sister? A sister who likes to have her hair just so, but will insist (if you comment on it) that her hairstyle matters not? A sister who waves her odd hands in front of you like a flock of wounded birds? A sister who will be something someday, partly by her own efforts, but mostly by yours? I have such a sister. She has had her likeness taken, and now professes to like it not. "The likeless," or "the lifeless," she calls it, calling of course all attention to herself. I admit, it is a flat, prim, unsubtle, unyielding, wooden thing, except for a trace of her humor, playing about her lips that don't quite smile. Neither does my mother smile, and she has had her likeness made, as well. I trust you have a mother, and will be able to imagine how tenderness is not the camera's gift. But a sister! You would have done sisters everywhere a favor had you kept your invention under wraps. I now have two sisters: the one who poses forever a martyr to the one who posed.

You realize you have taken one step too many

up the side of the limestone cliff in pursuit
of a wildflower barely three inches tall.
The stones and dead leaves are slick
with spring rain. To break an ankle here
would be inconvenient—someone on the trail
might hear your screams of pain—assuming
you didn't hit your head as well. How young
it looks, your hand against dark gray stone,
an odd pale fern the field guides never mention.
How young it looks, surrounded by all that isn't
hand: moss, leafless trees, geese in nesting pairs,
snail shells at water's edge, the flower so small
on the forest floor, yet trembling in the wind.

The Monson Ladies' Prayer Circle

What has many mouths, but is of one mind.
Eyes everywhere, and ears that can detect
unspoken thoughts. A thousand aunts
and cousins. Here is the church, here
is the steeple, open the door and—

and we do not know at first that one
is capable of such high treason,
that sweet face, the tender ministrations—

Emily is named a member of the third degree,
the first being saved,
the second, a possibility,
the third, without hope—

she becomes the lost cause
the Monson Ladies' Prayer Circle covets,
a gentle cousin of ours the go-between,
the tattler (Emily bristles at such a common word,
a third-degree word, she calls it)

and it is the beginning of her inwardness,
her capacity for secrets. The soul learns
that when one has a door, one keeps it closed.

Emily Writes from School

They have entrusted the knives to my care.
Imagine me, collecting dagger after dagger

gleaming as I traverse the large dining hall.
Perhaps they know better than to assign me forks,

for I should be too pointed. Or spoons,
for I should covet every drop. Knife after knife

passing through my slim hands.
The gleam seems to me sharper

than the blade, though I have promised
not to test that theory.

Knowing Emily

There is nothing she dislikes more intensely
than jostle. If she could go to market at midnight,

assured of being the only person out and about,
perhaps she would embark. Today we sit and watch

the rain, but after a few minutes she stands
and says, How the drops do crowd one another,

and she's off to find a book, although
the light's too soft for reading.

The Binding is Spoiled by Placing the Open Book Pages-Down

I will send you a length of ribbon
for a marker, she writes. Use it,
or never again will I lend you
any book of mine.

Perhaps the Queen will deign
to send a scroll, I reply—

A Certain Kiss

Just on the soft inside of the elbow, say.
Say it is the first warm day of spring.
A light perspiration dampens the skin.
The longing for sunlight fulfilled
would be enough, but there is this, too,
warmth upon warmth. Was it even
a kiss at all, one may wonder
just seconds after it occurred. Half kiss,
half taste. A little extra flick of moisture
from those lips still there. Loving equally
the freckle, the blue vein.

Sometimes She Goes Too Far

I had burned my hand lifting the kettle from the stove—nothing serious, one more small wound after a day of small wounds. She chooses that moment to ask me, "What are you proudest of, Vinnie?" I am rubbing butter on the burn; I look up, not at her, not at anything, really—I just look up at the wall, but beyond it, beyond this room, beyond this day, beyond Amherst, beyond anything I have ever or will ever know. She must have realized immediately that she has gone too far, has asked me for something impossible. When I think to look around, she has disappeared from the kitchen, and I am alone. I hear my own voice, barely a whisper—"That I have loved and still do love, in secret and in silence."

First Loss

It was understood. We had an understanding. The blue veins
in my wrist look like they form an "X," as if they meet and fuse,
before branching off and continuing each on its own. Emily says
that is not possible, for how would the blood know where to
go—it would not be efficacious, was her word. The veins must
just approach one another, perhaps cross, but not join as one.
Emily and I studied my wrist by candlelight, by the light of our
brightest lamp, and then by sunlight in the garden. We wanted
to see within, without disarming me. But that is what it must be,
the vessels at one point meeting but not mingling—

and that is what it must be, our understanding, true at one point,
then not, and the parting no more than the approach, and no
mingling of the contents. Each leaves—one leaves—still fully one.

Election

—Father is now a Legislator.
—But he has been one all along.
—But it is now the People's will.
—Alas.

Poor Maggie Tulliver

—We are submerged, each one of us.
—No, Emily, it cannot be so!

We whisper about death by drowning, how long one tries to hold out, the mundane discomfort of being soaked through weighed against the horror of the moment. We are glad we live as far from the river as we do, its meanders rearranged with each spring thaw. We are glad we live in a dry house rather than a dank mill. There's the poor miller of Montague, we say, thinking of his daughters right now sleeping above the great always-turning wheel, their stream rising, rising—Never again will I gaze out on a rainy night and pretend the dark road is a river upon which I could sail away. This isn't true; I still long for that river, every midnight rain promising an escape it cannot possibly deliver. The Montague girls in their mill, the great gears turning, turning beneath them, one deep breath, one more, one more—

When You Are Broken at Last

Do not speak of the avalanche
that broke you. No one will believe,
looking at the pieces that remain,
that it began as a pebble dislodged
by a careless step. Listeners

will imagine a smooth white stone
if you say "pebble," like something
pocketed once on a winter beach.
Not the crushing jagged shard
you call "pebble," because "pebble"

is the only word your shattered mouth
can form. It began with a pebble, you
might be able to say. What you mean is,
I loved someone, and that person
loved me in return.

Distance. Ways to Make It:

Be in the kitchen to maintain distance from the men.

Be sent away to school. This is temporary, and loved most in retrospect. Oh studies, forgive me; how I neglected you.

In writing, use turns of phrase, such as *appears content . . .* , *may call upon . . .* —language pulled in at the seams. This helps one allude to what once was normal, with little chance anyone will see past the formality.

Silence, where possible, without the closeness of questions.

And finally, forgetting.

What about forgiveness. I have gone some distance, trying to forgive my own enthusiasm. I allowed myself to misunderstand. The heart will imagine summer even as a killing frost descends.

Let us practice, then:

Last I heard, so-and-so was well. I have not had reason to call, nor do I think I shall. I doubt our paths, et cetera.

This Morning Belongs

to the wasp that stings me
and the weeds that refuse to give.

The vine whose taproot
defies all pulling, all digging.

The earthworms that surface and scatter
from the slicing spade.

The carpenter ants converting the barn
to sawdust. The spider who lives

beneath the broken shingle.
The catbirds, wrens, sparrows, crows.

This morning belongs to the crabgrass.
How can one not admire such persistence?

Tomatoes green and heavy on the vine.
Black-eyed susans tumbling across the path.

The wasp hiding in the folds of my sleeve,
displeased with the presence of arm.

This morning belongs to them all,
to their assurance of belonging,

their knowing how to endure.
More than endure. Flourish.

Seek-no-furthers

I love their name, but Emily will invent one
of her own: Constellations, for their pale spots
that look like stars in the night sky. Do not tell me

what will happen to the orchard after we're gone,
that someone would rather have lawn than apples,
or someone further on a tennis court. Seek not

too deeply into the future: one valley over from yours
drowned . . .
Why do you weep, Vinnie, Emily asks

when she finds me in the orchard. She transfers
the apples from my apron to hers, gentles me
back to the house. I try to tell her

what came to me, as if in a dream, the sun in my eyes
and the scent of apples lifting me out of this world
and into the next. Prescott, Dana, Enfield, Greenwich,

gone. A flood, Emily—
—Perhaps you saw the past,
Mr. Agassiz's glacier. Come, let's bake a pie

with your Seek-no-furthers, and cinnamon the house,
and we shall speak no more
of Noah and his sodden kin.

The Journey to Washington, D. C.

She clings; I cannot breathe.
She has me dreaming of a vast sea
of people, great waves of know-nothings

who will block one's every possible way.
I shall remain indoors, she vows,
and she is one to keep a vow.

What she means is, I shall not leave our room.
Me: I weep to think that Amherst will persist.
She notices a tear on my cheek and says,

This, too, shall pass. But it won't, I do not reply.
It will go on and on, forever. I mean Amherst.
It will pull us back. Swallow us alive.

Blasphemy

Mine will be the heaven of those
who loved in secret, loved in silence.

His will be the heaven of those
who squandered love, squandered time—

the two great sins, the reasons angels weep—
but a certain sector of heaven no doubt awaits

those who chose that pitiful path,
too weak for any other way.

Perhaps I shall take a turn around the parlor
on God's arm, there in my bold heaven.

Let him watch me stepping out. Let him watch
from his meek harp-dull cloud.

Please, Visitor, Do Not Tell

One spends her morning in the garden looking behind each lily, hoping to find something other than lily.

One indulges a peculiar fascination with flies.

From enigma to abyss, and back again.

As if trying to discern what they are thinking, the flies.

As if each had a message for her, the lilies.

Even when they are all in the same room, they are in different rooms.

That one has a wicked tongue, and you will laugh and laugh.

An incorporeal shadow descends the stairs, crosses through the library, and slips into the conservatory. You will watch and watch for this shadow, but you will miss it every time.

After they read a newspaper, there is nothing left—I swear they drink the print from off the page.

Better to have been born a flower, in that family. More attention that way.

Even with their repositioned doors, they cannot find a way out.

One is made of granite, yet somehow moves.

One is made of clouds, yet somehow holds quite still.

One is made of little frowns, frowns for shoulders, frowns for spine, frowns for frowns.

One is made for better things, but will be all Amherst in the end.

One seems made to live in the shadows of shadows.

Fossils

> *Surely it needs a professor of natural theology in our theological seminaries, (and if such chairs existed in our colleges they would be serviceable,) to teach those who expect to be officers in the sacramental host how to carry on the holy war.*
> —Edward Hitchcock, *Religion of Geology and Its Connected Sciences*, 1854

Dr. Hitchcock is a normal man
in that he loves cake. He talks
of giant birds who left their prints
in our great valley, just before
the Flood, heeding Noah's call
but dawdling over some irresistible
morsel (here he lifts another forkful
to his mouth) and the valley
turned to mud, and then to lake,
and here we now have great slabs
as testimony to what may happen
if we linger, tarry, indulge.

We were children. Moral lessons
were everywhere. Linger, tarry,
indulge—this is what happens
to anyone less than Doctors of Divinity
who enjoy their gingerbread too much.
Mother gave us *that look*, and off
we went to bed, where great birds
that missed the Ark somehow
found us, imperfect morsels
that we were, and carried us away
past dreams, past Ararat, leaving
not a trace of us behind.

Embroidered Tapestry

Plums. They look like plums, piled high
in a bowl, offered by the woman in robes
to the man in the comfortable seat. Some
with light skin, some dark, the plums,

which are also tossed across the hall
by jugglers, over the head of the man—
let us call him the Prince. He seems
delighted with the jugglers, a respite

from the duties of being Prince, and he
has ordered that more plums—more,
more!—be supplied to the jesters,
and when the trees are stripped of plums,

then peaches, quinces, apples, lemons,
until the jugglers drop from exhaustion,
die from thirst, the Prince thinking at first
it is part of the act, that now they will juggle

with their feet, lying on their backs,
not noticing too that the woman in robes
has long since run off with the overseer
of the orchard, the orchard bereft of fruit.

Imagining Emily

When she leaves the room, I think: Certainly I must have imagined her. Sunday was the first day warm enough to have the windows open, and she told me that her first thought as the church bells began to ring was, What is that cacophony? It is man's music, not God's, she continued, seeing my shocked expression. And she turned and walked out of the room. She would not believe me if I tried to explain why her words shocked me: I, too, have wondered about the cacophony of bells, what God would be made glad by it. She is possessive of her words, "cacophony" being a current favorite. It isn't mine to use.

Riddles

She'll thief a word and not so much as blush.
Allude to a far-off place and she'll out-location you.
She miracles it every time a robin sings.
She laws where others merely rule.

How to sister the one who sisters all?
Every smile's a smuggle, every morning a revive.
She reluctants time into parcels of nonce
then turns around and becomes the describe.

Watch her unletter an envelope: Oh surgeon,
please take such care with me!
She darks the day and lamps the night
and pencils the history of our grief.

Hard Freeze

Just one more day, she says.
I haven't said a word calling forth this
or any other response, so she may
not even be addressing me. Who, then?
The feather; the season; the impending freeze.
She carefully drapes a blanket over the rosebush.

I would have tried fire, several little fires,
here and there in the garden, hot coals
carried out from the house, Martha following
in our wake, concerned for
her good cast iron skillets.
I am a bringer of warmth—

But even as I write this, I forget
whose heart was for blankets,
whose for flames.

Variations

Autumn dons its finest dress

Autumn dons a yellow dress

My sister dons a yellow dress

My sister shuns a yellow dress

My sister shuns so many things

We shun so many things in life

We shun our lives and bid farewell

In dreams we dare to don our lives

We save our lives to live some day

Our lives like this, put by 'til Spring

Our lives like this, safely put away

Put up—put by—put back—put off—

One day we'll want them, these little lives

Not like this, encased in glass

Undonned, undonable, undone

Can you imagine us, encased in glass

Talking to Myself

Tell me about the sun that has not yet risen.

Tell me about the irises that will bloom in three, four months.

Tell me how, on some distant mountain,
a stone will slide a few feet down a slope
and come to rest upon another that will slide the night before.

Tell me how my heart will beat this way tomorrow.

Purple velvet, ice blue, butterscotch – the irises.

I love your lists. Make a list for me.
A bottle labeled "artificial tears."
The prism after the sun goes down.

Last season's nest woven fast to the branch.

The counterweight at the end of the window sash.

Name for me the grasses in the field. Make up names
for those birds in last night's dream.

Flower-breasted warbler, tawny thrush.
How someone in the dream, not you,
reached out and almost touched one.

Tell me about the carriages going by on Main Street.

And yellow—I forgot—the yellow irises, too many,
where did they all come from?

Tell me your unspoken thoughts. Let me read unwritten poems.

A Riddle for Sue

Poor Sue.
Pursue poor Sue.
Peruse poor Sue.
Per use. Poor Sue,

poured over,
word after word,
poem by poem,
made into one of us.

But that's impossible.
Sue knows it;
Emily will learn
the heartbreak way.

Pursue, pursue;
nothing Emily will not do,
word by word,
letter after letter.

Poor Sue,
perused.
She will grow
to hate us all.

Everything in Those Days Meant to Bind

the ribbon
around her throat
as if she were a pet bird

pintucks—
the handmade dress
made to outlast the model

dreadful steeple
beneath whose angles
angels

a serpent wonder:
is there really
any home for me?

one weed out of ten
good long taproot
still intact

Ssshhh ... merely whisper this: *hankering, gross, mystical, nude*

—with lines from *Leaves of Grass*

How could it not have been thus:
One sister obtains from a suitor
(oh yes! for suitors we both have)
a copy of a smallish book, banned
and therefore coveted

and one day Father and Mother take
their favorite drive to Monson,
and the house is ours
windows open to a warm breeze
secrets just begging to be born

the smallish book held open
between the sisters
every word consumed
—storm clouds never thought to fly
as fast as eyes across these pages—

and when they finish,
they turn back to the first lines
and read it through again.
    Is this then a touch? quivering me
    to a new identity ...

How could it not have been thus,
as it has been with sisters always,
this sharing of whispered things,
this Do you think it's so?
and I have felt it must be so.

We both can recite the sermons.
We both can fathom shame.
But Mr. Whitman answers:
> *Logic and sermons never convince,*
> *The damp of the night drives deeper into my soul.*

Where the one whose book it is
hides the book, I will never tell.
And how could those words
not become, somehow, my own:
> *Did it make you ache so, leaving me?*

"Emily, what does it mean?"

If you ask her that, she'll go all rigid in the shoulders,
and not show you anything she's written for a long time thereafter.

So one doesn't ask. One reads, and reads again.
At least they are short.
One can read and reread in an instant,
and appear thoughtful.

Let me consider its beauty, Emily,
I have learned to say.

It means so much—
The day I said that, she danced a little jig-like step.

I meant, I am overwhelmed by your words, Sister.
They oppress.

I don't say that out loud.
Only, when she interrupts me as I race a summer storm,
closing windows before a sideways rain reaches
the inner corners of each room—

The inundation is almost upon us. Oh but look,
you have a poem.

Gaze for Which I Ceased to Live

on a crumpled scrap
she has penciled
this strange phrase

and it helps me find a way
to emerge into the changed world
amazed at

its exorbitant use of color
its profligate sky
its easy warmth

where each inhalation
has nothing whatsoever
to do with you

she could not
have known
that she was writing

my liberation
which makes me realize
she must

have been
writing
her own

Gettysburg

As the newspaper describes it, a town
not unlike Amherst in terrain,
though no doubt a bit less straitlaced.

A few each week return by train,
boys, or what remains of them,
a leg or arm fewer here and there.

I heard one shout a phrase or two
at odd intervals, apropos of nothing—
cordwood, sister, stacked like cordwood—

they hurried him off to some
outlying farm. Perhaps he had been
Austin's substitute, the five hundred

long since spent. But Gettysburg.
The wounded taken into almost
every house, the paper says.

No doubt some recluse privileges
revoked. They have meadows, too.
For bobolink, substitute crow.

Alternate Words: Leaving/Staying

nothing can keep summer from _____

second brood, the catbirds _____

Must I invent my own words for leaving, for staying?
Everything leaves, almost nothing stays.
Lasts, yes, but not stays. Lingers, persists, haunts.
Insists, insisters.

But I am looking for staying,
a "stay" that will do in a poem
what the "stays" in the corsets
of our mothers' generation
did for their posture, snug
around one's torso, little room to breathe
and less to slouch, stays to keep what leaves
and what has perhaps already left
girdled by memory.

Stays to keep my nouns like ribs
aligned and ordered:

summer
catbird
hedgerow
nest

Each where it should be for
some improbable span of time
before it up and leaves,
before it up and stays.

Sense

Someday touch may be my last remaining sense
if the old women of Amherst are any forewarning

living out their days on boiled squash oatmeal
meat put through the grinder twice

their senses going one by one
taste smell eyes ears

I will miss scent most
In the garden today a rose

reminds me of the boy I loved
next to whom I loosened my hair

but that rose
a sweetness more like food than flower

nourishment—the thing I lost
when I lost all hope of him

odd to have that here so close at hand
a little trick of nectar and dew

so close at nose, Emily might write
loving the look of those words on the page

Samuel

It is the prerogative of one unmarried sister
to ask the other, "Is it quite wicked to observe
that all men marry badly?" Her sister nods.

They are baking gingerbread, expecting guests,
a married couple: the husband, a favorite
in their house, able to discuss world affairs

as if every sleepy Massachusetts borough
has a vital stake, able to make the sisters' father
not smile exactly—he never smiles—but raise

a corner of his mouth with something
not too far removed from incipient delight.
But then there is the other, the wife.

Starer at floors, utterer of "yes" or "no,"
no more than these two syllables to be drawn
forth. They have ten children, but it is not

the prerogative of one unmarried sister
to ask the other anything concerning this.
Though each sister, in her secret heart,

asks much concerning this, and much
about marriage, so many woeful ones
have they seen in their small sphere.

Abiah, with Dandelions in Her Hair

Because my sister loved her, I loved her too, with a younger sibling's adoration of all the elder holds dear. When Abiah left town without a visit, Emily sat up all night, as if resolved to never sleep until she saw that face. Or perhaps she hoped Abiah might appear below her window, and silent recognition might be exchanged. When does one stop expecting a proper knock on the front door and begin instead to fancy a figure half-lit by the stars to be standing at the edge of the road? I imagine myself the windowpane, cold barrier of hope between desire and absence. What a terrible, common lot in life it must be, to be the one who does not return another's love.

Anachronism: What Was Wrong with Her?

The diagnoses begin. Social phobia,
anxiety, agoraphobia. Phobia, phobia, phobia.
Say the word a few times, and it begins
to lose all meaning—a game known to children
since forever. The diagnoses change
with the times. Asperger's. On the spectrum.
Everyone has a theory. Every scholar wishes
for a drop of blood, a molar, an eyelash.
Even better than a diary: some DNA.
Seizure disorder. Consumption. Bipolar.
The exotic and the quaint. Homesick
even while at home. Sensitive.
Disappointed in love.
None of the above.

Riddles for Ned

I have flown, but I cannot fly.
I am barbed, but soft am I.
I offer lift, though I may be down.
I am the quill that makes this known.

❦

So many colors, my name is red,
A war of me left princes dead.
You love me with both nose and tongue
But to love me best I might draw blood.

❦

I require light, to throw it back.
Water or silver may suffice
though breeze or tarnish negates all.
I tell rough truths. I'm smooth as ice.

❦

I hold water from no earthly well.
I hold sky, but never blue.
I can hold nothing, but I point the way
To the point that is always true.

Fire in the Heart of Town

Bells, and smoke, and shouts. Our house too close!
The air affright with embers. A celebration,
the Fourth of July, I had to say to Emily,
to myself, really, had to say it's just the revelry

got out of hand. But those embers! Near-certain loss
of every cherished thing. Think what we'd know
of a certain poet's work if one ember, one
dauntless spark, had found a willing eave—

Conversation with the Butcher

—for Billy

His blood-splattered apron. Look him in the eyes.
He asks me if I have noticed the days growing shorter,
that it is dark by eight, though the calendar insists
we're still in summer. A eulogy for the waning season,
from this man for whom cold could be an advantage.
I do not like the darkness, he admits, tying a bow
on my parcel of bones for soup. Down to my marrow
I dread the early dark. 'The unimaginable touch of Time,'
your Mr. Wordsworth of England calls it. Cleaver
in the chopping block. Eat slowly. Eat slowly, he says,
and partake. To him, the word connotes something
beyond sustenance. Something more akin to grace.

Emily Bakes Gingerbread for Cousin Zebina, Which I Take to Him While Emily Sits with Mother

I have dreams of walking. Last night, I climbed
Mount Holyoke, a trail so steep at times
I saw my outstretched arm, I saw my hand
take hold of trees to pull myself along.
My hand was strong, and I was walking.
And I reached the summit, and looked down
on the great ox-bow of our River. But oh,
what happened next: Out over it all, out
over the whole great green expanse of vale
I went, like a bird. Take this little verse
of mine to Emily, to thank her for all of hers.
Tell her it's the epitaph I'll never have:
Here sleeps Zebina Montague.
He walketh not, but his spirit flew.

Cousin Zebina's Paralysis

He set off to see the world.
How he made it home he only
half remembers. He thinks
he was carried part-way
by a kind stranger, about whom
Cousin Zebina says he dreams
sometimes, almost remembering
the man's features, deep-set
eyes too far apart, hooked nose,
and maybe it was only for a mile,
this journey in a stranger's arms,
but still, *the things I tell him
in those fevered dreams,*
Cousin says, shaking his head.
*How we set off to see the world,
and lose it all, and come home
to prepare ourselves to lose the rest.*

What Can Be Found

I will be known as the finder of things.
There is no such thing as "lost," I say,
and I turn around, and there it is,

the unexpected item in an unexpected spot.
Where the cat has disappeared
to have her kittens. Where the rose clippers

share secrets with the hand saw.
I saved Troy from the Greeks, it seems,
such was the import of my locating

the featherduster behind a bureau.
Keys and handkerchiefs. Names.
Last season's like-new gloves.

Lost is not the same as gone.
A thing that is gone is with us
in all new ways.

Prone to Outbursts

Do I say to him, making my voice
as small as possible, How did you
make such a mess of things?

All your knowledge of the law,
all your ability in ordering the affairs
of others, for knowing the best course—

and here you are, shouting at me,
or shouting at the room in general,
because of a broken buckle or some other

inconsequential thing, something
that would upset a child—no, something
that would make a child laugh, but you

it sets off as if you have just this moment
realized that your son and daughter despise you,
that the child who died young is better off,

the house our father built to bribe you
sags beneath the weight of bitterness,
its florid wallpaper, once the height of fashion,

now a reminder of how things remain the same
on the surface yet suffocate with time.
I say nothing, except Austin, oh Austin.

The Yellow Day

—September 6, 1881

Emily and I came out to the garden to feel the charred air. People needed lanterns at noon. Some spoke of Judgment Day, sat down in their houses (it was impossible to stay outdoors for long) to await the rapture. Fires to the west, of course, the less-superstitious well knew, after the year's bad drought. Secretly, though, we wonder if we are on our way to heaven, or—

The Mushroom Girl

When she comes to the back door with her basket, she tells me how she has been out walking since before the sun was up. She measures distance in hours—four hours from town, four hours back, plus time spent foraging, her gaze groundward, scanning the ferny woods, gathering mushrooms, sorrel, wild onions. Except once, she tells me (and I listen!) ahead of her on the path someone kicked a stone, and she looked up and saw his eyes, the boy who works in the quarry, who wants to learn to carve headstones, so he'll never, as he told her, be wanting work. And so that day a basket of golden chanterelles overturns near a sun-warmed place, and a few tumble out to the base of the fern that arches over and brushes the top of her head.

Judge Otis Phillips Lord (1812–1884)

Judge Lord: What a moniker, each half
vying for oppressiveness with the other.
When we were children and he'd visit,
I'd think, This is what it would be like
to have two Fathers. And so of course,
of course, dear Emily goes and falls
in love. What is it with some women—
Emily with her sour Salem, Mabel
with dark and dour Austin—what is it
draws them to these shadow men,
men misremembered by life's prime?
I have had it up to here with gravitas.
Laugh, you toothless lion, let in
what little remaining light you'll know
before earth fills in the space between
those parchment lips. She thought,
my sister, that I was angry
that she might go away. I wasn't even
that far ahead to what might happen
should they marry. I couldn't think
past the horror that she'd waste herself,
bride of Death, on him—redundant gloom,
double drear, twin miseries. It cured me,
thinking of that icy touch, of all
the heartache of all these years.
Made me see that loneliness is a blessing,
an ardent companion, always willing,
always supple, always new.

After Burning All Her Letters

All the familiar handwriting, each swirl and dash, each open "a," each fishhook "j," every elongated dot above an "i" like a flame above a tiny candle—all those candles, all those tiny flames—

They were addressed to her, but it was my life being consumed. Good-bye, Samuel, good-bye dear cousins, farewell Helen. Good-bye again to many of you—it was as if you died twice, this time by my own hand, page after page into the flames, a conflagration of words, tears burning my cheeks.

Why, sister, why did I do it? Why do you ask such things? Why had you not burned them yourself, rather than squirrelling all these words away? You and your fortune. Your fortune, the anguish of those left behind.

I did the letters first, then turned to your poems. Should those go into the flames as well?

No.

Turns out, I find my own way to defy.

April, 1886

— Do you remember once, I said to you, Some day we shall be old women in this house.

—You never said any such thing.

—I thought it, then, and only dreamed I told you. I foresaw this day. You bathing me. The water hurts.

—Is it too hot?

—It is water, and it hurts. Have you been to the garden?

—This morning, to see the lilies.

—I wish we could walk in the woods. The morels must be out.

—Gone by now, I'd think.

—And the mosses green, the different mosses. We promised we'd learn their names.

—Let's make up our own, as we did for birds and flowers.

—Belle-o'-the-brook.

—Clover hearts.

—Lovers' pillow.

—Forest blush.

—Mountain tears.

—Is that moss or fern?

—I thought we were doing ferns.

—You are tired, and should rest.

—Will you go to the garden without me?

—My garden is here.

Judgment Day

We awaken and rise toward glory, our bodies
not bodies but something better, a secret
the angels tumble over themselves to reveal

but even more wonderful is how we all
meet one another again, look into
each other's eyes that are better than eyes

recognize those we have not seen
since we, since they, were young, recognize even
the great-great-grandchild we never knew in life

those who loved as one
those who never met
sharing now the wings of eternity

and those tumbling angels
all ungainly, unloosed spirit—
won't Heaven be better for our presence

When I Bathed Them

Mother after her stroke,
then Emily, bedridden
(although she whispered, please
do not use that word of me)

the sound of water filled
the room, wrung from the sponge
back into the bowl. A living sound.
A sound like laughter.

It made them both smile.
As there was little else
to do, I bathed their arms
and shoulders 'til they shone.

My fingers ached with wringing,
but how could I complain.
A liquid gesture. We will meet again,
water into water, crystal clear.

Parts of Us

his lungs this time
his poor body
piece by piece

mustn't wake the house
all night
her mouth full of blood

so much sugar
is this really good for us
hummingbird

summer sky
how small you are up there
vulture

dragonfly
the emerald eyes
you see just once

falling sickness
is anything broken
other than sense

uncommon sweetness
the mathematician hip deep
in ferns

and that one's heart
we thought it had broken
years ago

Ordinary Deaths in an Ordinary Family

Each death makes the paper. Our roster
of those who perish in the war with one
who always wins.

News of Father's death arrived by Father's train.

Mother's slow decline, unable to leave her bed.
Her eyes at the end, moving, moving,
as if there were dozens of us in the room.

I will not write what happened next.

No, Lavinia, you must.
Ned. Our boy. *A Promising Boy*,
the newspaper called him. As if
the entire commonwealth
were trying to comprehend.

Even to go to market after that.
Pity like the sting of bees.

And then.
And then.

Sister. Brother.

Another one too young,
and with him, this branch
of the family name.

Down to this.
I wait.

In a Few Years, It Will Be the Twentieth Century

Think of it, I say to the ghosts in the house.
They do not like to think of it.
The ghost of Mother leaves the room.

Father's ghost finds ways to stomp
his disapproval: a heavy book tumbles
off a shelf, a door slams when there is

no breeze to slam it. Austin's ghost
sits and broods, a cold authority
midway up the stairs. He takes my arm

and makes me sit, breathless. Austin,
I tell him, you are worse than Emily,
spending all your time neither

up nor down. Modern times, Austin!
Just think what we might have seen, had we
been born a little later, lived a little longer.

There is talk of flying! But then I find I am
alone. They do not want to hear such things,
my ghosts. They prefer the past.

'Round they go, in constant search
of it, laughter long silenced,
a perpetual Sunday gloom.

And So It Is

And so it is that a small thing happens.
A dragonfly takes a gnat on the wing,
lands on a spent lily stalk to feed.

The low sun reddens the dragon's wings,
causes you to notice the entire
winged world, going down to autumn.

Even the yellow walnut leaves look
like winged things. Even our love,
years and years in the making,

year after flying year, even our love
takes wing, and into this small
enormous world is lifted, borne aloft.

Summer, 1899

Horseless carriages will one day make Amherst even smaller. And we will fly soon, they say. Men are contriving such miracles. Soon, *soon*, everything is always in those wondrous days of soon, the word on everyone's lips.

Girls are becoming educated despite the railing of fathers, the handwringing of mothers.

I let the garden go a little, after you were called back. I hadn't the heart to pull the sisters of the weeds you'd pulled.

I may have made you somewhat famous. I'm sorry, and not sorry. Even your scrawls on scraps are revered.

Who knows, Emily, but that in some strange future, the garden may live again. The hummingbird generations!

 **Jean LeBlanc** grew up in Massachusetts, just about halfway between Emily Dickinson and Henry David Thoreau. She now lives in northwestern New Jersey with her husband and best friend, George Lightcap. She has taught writing and literature at Sussex County Community College since 1999, and is a member of several local poetry groups: the Writers' Roundtable of Sussex County; the Paulinskill Poetry Project; and the Silconas Poetry Center (of which she is a past director). Her publications include poetry anthologies as well as collections of her own work. Her poetry advocates for an awareness of the beauty of this journey called life.

Shanti Arts

Nature ▪ Art ▪ Spirit

Please visit us online
to browse our entire book catalog,
including poetry collections and fiction,
books on travel, nature, healing, art,
photography, and more.

Also take a look at our highly regarded art
and literary journal, *Still Point Arts Quarterly*,
which may be downloaded for free.

www.shantiarts.com

www.ingramcontent.com/pod-product-compliance
Lightning Source LLC
Chambersburg PA
CBHW051607170426
43196CB00038B/2954